Rowing
with
One Oar

Lessons in Delivering
Greater Value
—— While ——
Remaining Competitive

John Regep

ARCHWAY
PUBLISHING

Archway Publishing books may be ordered through booksellers or by contacting:

Archway Publishing
1663 Liberty Drive
Bloomington, IN 47403
www.archwaypublishing.com
1 (888) 242-5904

ISBN: 978-1-4808-5918-0 (sc)
ISBN: 978-1-4808-5919-7 (hc)
ISBN: 978-1-4808-5920-3 (e)

Library of Congress Control Number: 2018903507

Print information available on the last page.

Archway Publishing rev. date: 04/03/2018

ACKNOWLEDGEMENT

To my sister, Marie Regep, for her talents and contribution of illustrations in this book.

Contents

INTRODUCTION

We have all at one time or another faced the requirement to "Do more with less," and while we struggle with these two opposing directives within the realm we control, we see other teams spend time, energy, and dollars on new processes, consultants, or software that don't have a logical chance of improving the company's bottom line. In many companies, large and small, when failures occur (departmental or individual), the proposed solution is often to layer on additional, people, steps, and bureaucracy, which leads to increases in staff and expenses. If left unchecked, the result is too many people and not enough ownership of the outcomes. Furthermore, teams will find themselves working hard and doing their jobs yet not getting anywhere.

I once used the analogy "it's like rowing with one oar" to describe what I was observing within my group. That phrase kept churning in my head over and over again while on a family vacation. Over thirty years of business experiences and outcomes kept coming to the surface of my thoughts. I couldn't relax until I sat down and wrote the short story "The One Oar Rowboat." It only took about an hour to write, requiring only minor changes during my proofreading when I returned to work (which I wish I spent a little more time doing).

On August 12, 2016, I posted the story on LinkedIn. It's a

fictional account of a process that goes out of control and way off the scales of any measurement of Return on Investment (ROI). It is written in a screenplay format and is reproduced in the next chapter, slightly edited from what was originally published. The story was met with immediate comments and "likes" because it rang true for so many readers. If anything in this story rings true for you, then you should look at the story's message as an area for improvement that should be investigated.

I'm sometimes asked if the story pertains to any particular incident or company. I reply that, like most stories, it is a composite of many different experiences put together into one fictional storyline to make a point and tell an exciting story. If you see any of these behaviors at your current job, you are one step closer to making a positive difference!

Although the story is a bit tongue in cheek, it is meant to be not only a serious look at today's world of consulting, management and employee retention but also a view at the current trend of diving in head first into new products or processes without a stated goal, an analysis of ROI, or a definition of the criteria for success. All too often, changes are made without the proper engagement of all interested parties and without gaining "buy-in" from stakeholders. Success should be defined at the beginning of a project, or else any result can be proclaimed a success.

I thought it might be helpful, to those seeking to improve to go through each of the "actors'" lines and expand on the hidden message(s). So, in chapter 2, I present my analysis of what I might have meant while writing it.

> *"Success should be defined at the beginning of a project, or else any result can be proclaimed a success."*

ORIGINAL POST

LinkedIn, August 12, 2016

The One Oar Rowboat

J Regep

Boss: *Okay. Now just like before, let's row to those islands. I'll stay on the dock and give directions, you jump in and start rowing, and I'll let you know which island as soon as I find out where the business wants to go.*

Employee: *This rowboat only has one oar.*

Boss: *That's the latest and greatest oar! It's the newest technology! Lighter, larger surface area, and three times as fast as the old ones. And it requires only half the effort.*

Employee: *But this rowboat is designed for two oars.*

Boss: *Do the math: you should be able to go 50 percent faster with the same effort.*

Employee: *What?*

Boss:	*Just get in and start rowing—we have a deadline.*
Employee:	*Okay, but—*
Boss:	*Go left. Go left!* GO LEFT!
Employee:	*I am going left! My left.*
Boss:	*But you're just going around in circles. We need a consultant.*
Consultant:	*The correct term is "starboard." If you say that, even though the rower is facing you, you both will know what direction each of you is talking about. In nautical terms, while facing forward toward the bow (that's the front), the left side is called port, and the right is starboard.*
Boss:	*Wow! You really know your stuff. I need someone like you around here.*
Consultant:	*Cha-ching!*
Boss:	*Go starboard! Go starboard!*
Employee:	*What? You mean left?*
Boss:	*No. My left, your right. It's called "starboard." Don't you know anything?*

Employee: *Okay, but the oar is on the wrong side. I'll have to stop and switch it.*

Boss: *Okay, but hurry up; we are running out of time.*

Employee: *Okay, done.*

Boss: *But now you're going around in circles the other way! We need that consultant.*

Consultant: *What you need is a rudder and a helmsman at the stern (that's the back) to steer the boat in the right direction. I can sell you a rudder and get an experienced helmsman.*

Boss: *Wow! You really know your stuff. What else can we do? We are really behind our schedule.*

Consultant: *Well, many nautical shops have a navigator at the bow with a compass, electronic sextant, GPS, and charts. It's industry best practice. I can get you those too.*

Boss: *Do it. ASAP.*

Consultant:	Cha-ching!
Boss:	Get back to the dock. We have to start all over. We need a rudder installed. And make room for a helmsman and a navigator and some other equipment.
Employee:	What? Why?
Boss:	Don't ask questions! Just do it. I have a consultant who knows what he's doing.
Consultant:	Everything is installed, and we are ready to go.
Boss:	Okay! Everyone in the boat! Let's go!
Employee:	There's not much room here—and the boat is pretty deep in the water. We are taking in water. It's hard to row.
Boss:	Just go! We are way behind schedule! We need that consultant.
Consultant:	I can get a couple of guys from offshore. They have master's degrees in electronic engineering, but we trained them in rowing. They are really strong; one can row during the day, and the other can row at night. You'll need a second shift helmsman and navigator too. Oh, I see water in the boat. You could use a bilge pump too.

Boss: Do it! **We are behind schedule.**

Consultant: **Cha-ching!**

Boss: **Okay! Everyone in the boat! Let's go! Toward that island! We need to get there yesterday!**

Consultant: Which island? We need a map. And some documentation on how you have been going to islands in the past.

Boss: I have an employee who doesn't understand this new technology. He can document what we used to do. Bring the employee back here to the dock. You manage the boat. We will stay here on the dock and document the process while you're rowing.

Employee: Hey, what's this other rowboat with only one oar doing tied to the dock?

Boss: *That's the DRB.*

Employee: *What?*

Boss: *Disaster recovery boat.*

Employee: *Can't I just use this oar and row the boat with two oars like we always did in the past?*

Boss: *Don't you know anything? Are you still living in the past? We need to have a backup in case the primary rowboat sinks. Besides, I have solved the problem; the consultants are succeeding where you failed. And now I have two rowers for the same price as one employee! Twice as far for the same price! I have improved productivity!*

Employee: *Hey, look. I can stand in the front (or in nautical terms, the bow) and use this one oar to paddle the rowboat—um, I mean DRB—on both sides like it's a canoe. And I can go pretty fast too.*

Boss: *Stop fooling around! Are you done with that documentation yet?*

Employee: *Hey, look. I can tie my shirt to this oar to create a sail and let the wind blow the rowboat. And I'm going really fast!*

Boss: *I told you to quit fooling around; you haven't completed the documentation yet. You're fired!*

Employee: *Too late. I quit. I got a job with a sailing company.*

This is an example of a win/win/win situation: The consultant made lots of money and has an indefinite engagement as the resident expert in all things nautical. The boss got a promotion for solving nautical problems. And the employee found a new career sailing instead of rowing.

ANALYSIS and LESSONS

Boss: *Okay. Now just like before, let's row to those islands. I'll stay on the dock and give directions, you jump in and start rowing, and I'll let you know which island as soon as I find out where the business wants to go.*

This starts out as just another day in the office; today's project shouldn't be any different from that of any previous day. The boss says, "Let's row" but intends to just watch the progress from the dock without actually doing any rowing or even getting into the boat. You may begin to wonder if the boss has ever rowed a boat before—or even been in one.

He sets the boat out without knowing the exact requirements. He knows it's going to be one of those islands, but he doesn't know exactly which one. Presumably, he feels he will figure it out before the boat has gone too far.

The line "as soon as I find out where the business wants to go" is a little dig at corporate management. It can be difficult to understand the corporate direction. While it is probably in the mission statement posted on a website, mission statements are often ambiguous and are, at best, generalities, not specifics.

They seem to make the senior leadership feel good but do very little toward making a company successful.

Before any project starts, the ultimate goal needs to be stated and known by all the concerned parties. Everyone needs to be rowing in the same direction with the same sense of urgency. But in practice, you will find that it is easier to be ambiguous; you can change your mind without admitting it, and you can claim a success when none exists.

Not knowing where you are going when you set out on a journey, costs your company money—money that is in short supply. If you make a course correction early, it won't be that big a cost, so many people think they are delivering faster if they start first and then get direction. But once you start, the urgency of defining the goal is gone. Without the urgency, it takes longer to decide, and the longer you wait, the further you go, and the further you go, the amount of course corrections you need to make increases exponentially.

These course corrections increase the timeframe and are viewed as schedule delays. At the end of the journey, those rowing the boat get blamed for the delays caused by the people who gave the directions at the start. Why? Because if you look at the end point and the starting point, the journey looks like a direct line; nobody remembers the zigzags that took place during the decision process. Does that sound familiar? Why does it continue to take place? Think how much more profit your company could be making with this one adjustment: Don't start a project without a defined, written goal.

Many leaders think they are being heroes by starting as early as possible, even before the goal is known. While intuitively, it may seem that they'll reach the goal sooner if they start sooner, in reality, as a process, this is the wrong thing to do.

First, as already mentioned, the urgency to get to a decision is gone. And second, the ownership gets lost. The rowing manager is now on the hook to deliver on time without even knowing where the team is going. The manager will be blamed when the boat doesn't arrive when it was needed, and no one will remember the extra time spent to make a decision. Competitive companies know the importance of keeping responsibilities where they belong and will ask the right questions when delivery dates are missed. They will find the root cause and make corrections.

"Don't start a project without a defined, written goal."

Employee: *This rowboat only has one oar.*

The employee is just stating a fact, not offering any other details or mentioning how this might affect progress—and definitely not offering any solutions. Obviously, the employee is just doing what he is told and not going beyond the job's duties.

Also, the employee is surprised: this is supposed to be just another day at the office—after all, the boss said, "just like before." Yet now there is only one oar! No one said anything about changing the number of oars. The boss has set the expectation that this row to the islands is just like previous efforts, but now there is something different.

One of the biggest hurdles to becoming competitive is that employees do only what they are told. How do you gain efficiency and continuous improvement if you don't encourage your people to ask questions and make suggestions? Employees should be mentored to go beyond stating the obvious and that they should expand their comments to include how a process affects them and the project. They also need to feel safe making recommendations. Bosses that won't listen to suggestions (or, worse, berate anyone who dares question their decisions) are not true leaders.

Have you ever worked where there was a suggestion box? Did it last very long? As part of the process, did the direct manager of the person putting in the suggestion review and analyze the suggestion and then come up with a recommendation? The boss probably felt that this was just another meaningless task that he had to perform, getting in the way of doing what he'd rather be doing. Interest in the suggestion box begins to dwindle as suggestions are not taken seriously, until it is finally removed. It shouldn't take a "box" to get suggestions from your workers; contributing new ideas and continuously evaluating processes and procedures should be regular habit of your team. Such behavior contributes to your company's consistent competitiveness. Perhaps starting with a suggestion box will get the juices flowing until it becomes normal to discuss improvements regularly and in an open forum where everyone can contribute ideas.

The employee isn't off the hook here either. He's assuming the boss knows more than he does. We are using the analogy of rowing with one oar. It's a simple situation, rowing with only one oar, and most people will understand it—but only most people. There are people out there who have never even been in a rowboat before, let alone one with only one oar that they are now required to row. In most business (and elsewhere), there are processes and procedures that are quite complex and involved. It can be difficult for an outsider to understand the ramifications of a simple fact like "This rowboat has only one oar."

All too often, people get promoted to a management position without ever doing the actual work that they are supposed to be managing. They may know the 'nautical' terminology, but they do not really understand the processes. Successful companies need experienced managers, ones that either come up through the ranks or, if hired from the outside, have experience doing the things they manage.

There are exceptions; some good managers instinctively know how to encourage others to perform well, and these managers quite often also know how to hire middle managers who do have the experience they lack. They trust their employees to know what they are doing and will give them the opportunity to make improvements. These exceptions also know how to listen to their employees and to learn from them, encouraging openness and constructive suggestions.

Leaders should bring their employees in on the decision-making process. It includes the employee, and if done properly, it gives the employee some ownership in the decision, which creates the motivation to succeed.

"Including employees in the decision-making process gives the employee some ownership, which create the motivation to succeed."

Boss:	*That's the latest and greatest oar! It's the newest technology! Lighter, larger surface area and three times as fast as the old ones AND requires only half the effort.*

It sounds like the boss is reading the glossy brochure from the sales presentation. The oar is lighter and larger than what? What proof is there that it is three times faster and requires only half the effort? Again, measured against what? Was there any "proof-of-concept" study performed? Was there any research into these claims?

A decision is made to bring in new technology, and the people who are to use it were not a part of the decision-making process. Not that everybody should participate, particularly in large companies, but they should know that there is a discussion taking place. They need to be allowed to contribute in some way and be kept abreast of the progress and timeline.

Productivity increases just by making the employees a part of the decision making. It's called the Hawthorne effect, from a study done at a Western Electric plant in Hawthorne, Illinois, in the 1930s. The company was trying to see if changes in the environment (heating, lighting, colors, etc.) would lead to increased productivity. They invited the employees to participate in the study, suggest changes, and discuss their effects.

What was found was that no matter what changes were made, productivity and morale increased! Further studies were done to understand why. They found that employee involvement was the key. It wasn't the changes themselves; it was the involvement. It still holds true today, but many managers learn it the hard way or not at all.

Employee: *But this rowboat is designed for two oars.*

Again, the employee is just stating the facts without men-
tioning how performance is affected or suggesting any solution.
Perhaps the employee believes the boss knows what he's doing.
More likely, he has been conditioned to not question the boss.
It happens all the time; employees are just doing what they are
told, not offering up suggestions.

Whose fault it that? The employee? Or their management?
A leader should coach the employee that what they are doing is
meaningful and efficient and listen to the employee if they feel
there might be a better way. It's okay to say, "Well, let's get this
done the current way, and then we can talk about improving
the process for the next time."

This is especially true if the task is short and there is some
urgency to finish. However, it's to your advantage to have the
discussion. Even if you feel the employee's suggestions are
wrong, that doesn't mean the current process is the best possible one. Always keep thinking of improvements and solicit
ideas; if nothing else, this involves the employee, who feels he
adds value. This has a positive effect on morale, which leads to
a positive effect on the company's bottom line.

Boss: *Do the math: You should be able to go 50 percent faster with the same effort.*

Apparently, the Boss has learned about oars from the salesman that sold him the oars. The boss most likely paid three times the price of a normal oar, but he doesn't reveal that part. Was it even in the budget or part of any capital improvement plan? Many companies nowadays don't require department heads to get approval of out-of-budget expenditures. The manager has "signing authority" up to a certain level and is trusted by his superiors to run his department his way. Maybe he justified the spending by an anticipated reduction in head count or got the money from some other project he never started.

Each and every project that is undertaken, whether in budget or not, should stand on its own and be approved by more than just the person with signing authority. He has "signing authority," but there should be a corporate policy in place that all purchases need to be justified, in writing, with stated purpose, needs, goals, and definitions of success.

For a company to remain competitive, every dollar spent needs to be offset by an increase in (profitable) revenue or a reduction in costs. These anticipated returns on investment need to be defined and measurable, and those who signed the contract that led to the expense need to be held accountable for any deviations (either bad or good).

Employee: *What?*

If two new oars are three times faster than two old oars, then one new oar should be one and one-half times better than two old oars. (2 N.O. = 3 x 2 O.O., 1 N.O. = 3 O.O.) What? One new oar is equal to three old oars. Regardless of the math, you can't get past the fact that the boat was designed with two oars in mind—changing the number of oars is not going to get the performance gains, regardless of how good the sales pitch was.

What is the salesman's motivation, is it reducing costs for your company or increasing sales for his? How can companies take the salesman's word for the benefits of their products? It's crazy how often the salesmen succeed! And even crazier is that companies rarely challenge the salesman (or his company). The salesman knows that the boss who signed the contract isn't likely to admit his mistake and will work like the devil to hide and deny any problems. This is how salesmen get away with it.

Not that all salesmen sell bad products. There are good products out there. However, competitive companies do their due diligence and properly vet new products. Ask around your company. Most likely, somebody has used this new oar, or knows someone who has. And don't just go with the recommendation of someone the salesmen led you to; remember, they might not want to admit that they were wrong. The best products are sold by companies that use their own product; they may even offer a total managed solution, with which they should be able to take over the "outcome and ownership" more cheaply than anyone else because their products are that good. The point here is that sales material is just that: sales material. It should never be taken as fact and definitely shouldn't be the only deciding factor.

Boss: *Just get in and start rowing—we have a deadline.*

The boss doesn't understand the math either; he's just going with what the sales guys told him. He believes that the rower should just get started rowing—how hard can that be? The sooner you start rowing, the sooner you will arrive, right? There's no time for training, practice, and things like that.

There is always a steep increase in costs when changes take place. You can't avoid it. You can ignore it, but you can't avoid it. If anyone tells you differently, then be suspicious of their qualifications. Are they just telling you what you want to hear? What are their motivations? Are they willing to take ownership and responsibility stating clearly that their budget won't increase? Are they going to put their bonus on the line? Or even their current job title? Rarely will you find someone willing to offer more than talk. It takes time to learn new systems and processes, and that costs money, but the rewards should eventually be lower costs (or greater sales), right?

The best time to make big changes is at the beginning of the fiscal year. This way, the learning curve is at the beginning of the budget cycle, and as you move through the year, you will see a performance increase, which should result in less costs and more revenue. So by the end of the year, your budget should be on the positive side of the balance sheet.

But if you wait until the beginning of the fiscal year, you have lost an opportunity by not starting right away. If you have a great idea, implement it as soon as possible. However, some companies do have strict budget guidelines, so waiting might be the only option. But at great companies, they are just that, guidelines.

Talk with your leadership and see if you can pitch your idea to those who make the budget decisions, and tell them that going over budget this year will mean fewer costs next year. Even if you don't get the go-ahead, you have primed the pump for the next budget cycle. If you don't try, it won't happen.

Employee: *OK, but—*

The employee doesn't have time to absorb the logic of "the math" but does understand that this isn't going to work. He just does his job as instructed. A definite culture is present that prohibits employee input.

This is why the idea of a suggestion box (or employee survey) is important. You must give your workers an opportunity to express their ideas; they know better than anyone else what is going on. They will also be honest if they feel secure. The problem is that most people don't know how to give constructive criticism or express themselves in a non-judgmental way. Therefore many managers get irritated if they have to listen to the line worker complain that they won't even give their workers the opportunity.

However, a good leader will learn the patience necessary to listen to *what* the worker has to say and not to *how* it is said. And a great leader will mentor their employee on how to get better at expressing themselves. The tried and true method of repeating back to a person what was said works well. It allows the leader to rephrase the idea, this time with a better, more constructive tone. The leader can show that he understands what the employee is trying to say and at the same times teach a new skill.

"A good leader will learn the patience necessary to listen to what the worker has to say and not to how he said it."

Boss: *Go left. Go left! GO LEFT!*

Imagine what it's like to row a boat with only one oar. The "push" of the oar happens on only one side of the boat, and the boat just goes in a circle. The boss does the only thing he knows, give directions, but doesn't know how to give instructions. He keeps repeating himself but expects a different outcome. He does increase his volume, more likely out of frustration than from trying something different. This boss doesn't know what it is like to row a boat, so he can't give any constructive commands; therefore, his options are very limited.

This manager should have taken it upon himself to learn something about rowing when he got this assignment to lead boat rowers. There is a wealth of information available today, free on the internet or in modestly priced books that can be purchased online or in stores. There is also training available, for reasonable prices, on just about every topic out there. If nothing else, the manager can hop in a boat and try out rowing himself. There is a lot of wisdom in the idiom "Before you judge a man, walk a mile in his shoes." This is true for leading, not just judging.

Employee: *I am going left! My left!*

The employee is finally showing some backbone by telling the boss he is following the boss's direction. He also gives some necessary information, but it comes in the form of an excuse, not as a constructive point. In real life, the employee might start shouting, "I'm doing what you told me to do!" or "This is all your fault." Or in this company's culture, he might just say those things to himself or to friends at lunch who aren't in any position to make changes to the situation.

Even if the employee comes off as rude or disrespectful, this doesn't mean there isn't something going on that needs to be changed. Whose fault is it when people start acting disrespectfully? Often, it's the employee who gets punished, even to the point of losing his job. But what was wrong in the environment that lead to the pressure that made the employee loss his temper in the first place? A good leader will coach an employee on how to express himself differently, he will also listen to what the employee is trying to say.

"A good leader will coach an employee on how to express himself differently; he will also listen to what the employee is trying to say."

Boss: *But you're just going around in circles. We need a consultant.*

The boss can only see the outcome of not getting where he wants to be. He is not able to understand the physics of rowing. It becomes obvious that the boss has never rowed a boat before or even observed the process. Makes you wonder how he got the job in the first place.

Nor does he understand the communication barrier that exists when two people have a confrontation. They can have completely opposite ideas of what "left" means. Again, we must ask: how did he get the job if he doesn't understand normal human-to-human interactions? All he knows how to do is to hire a consultant.

He could have read a book or taken rowing lessons. If there wasn't any time for this, he could have just had a conversation with the employee, but instead his company lets him hire a consultant. More than likely, his bosses are equally unsuited for managing boat rowers.

"When two people have a confrontation, they can have completely opposite ideas of what 'left' means."

Consultant: *The correct term is "starboard," That way, even though the rower is facing you, you both will know what direction you each are talking about. In nautical terms, while facing forward toward the bow (that's the front), the left side is called port, and the right is starboard.*

The consultant knows that it is very important to know all the latest and greatest terminology: this impresses people who don't know any better.

Boss:　　　*Wow! You really know your stuff. I need someone like you around here.*

The consultant has done nothing to solve the problem at hand but has demonstrated his vast knowledge of nautical terminology. People assume he is a seaworthy veteran, someone to be completely trusted to know the solution to any problem when it comes to rowing a boat.

Consultant: Cha-ching!

Success! The consultant has done his job: He is making money. He moves his hand as if he is working an old-fashioned cash register and imitates the sound "cha-ching!" He has convinced his client that he is smarter and more experienced than anyone else in the company when it comes to nautical matters.

If the employee had said more than just the facts when he said, "This rowboat only has one oar" and said something like, "This boat is designed for two oars; with only one oar, all the 'push' will be on one side and the boat will go in circles. Two oars create an even 'push' on both sides, which allows the boat to go in a straight line," perhaps the boss would have thought more highly of the employee.

However, the actions of the boss suggest that he doesn't have much respect for the employee, so he probably would have just dismissed anything the employee said. An employee should not only be comfortable speaking up. They should feel obligated to express the full story so that management can make informed decisions. The advice may not always be taken, but an employee should never feel that giving it would somehow harm their career.

Boss: ***Go starboard! Go starboard!***

Now the boss can demonstrate his vast knowledge of all things nautical, as well as his superior leadership qualities. Few people know that the more correct instruction would be "Change course to starboard" (with some indication of how many degrees). The boss looks smart because he used a fancy technical term, and nobody knows that he used it incorrectly.

Could this be why some bosses don't send their people to training? If the employee went to training, perhaps he would come to know more than the boss, and the boss would look bad. In reality, the boss looks good when all his people are highly qualified and trained, so why isn't training a higher priority at many companies? There is a "clique joke" out there that goes something like this: CFO says, "What happens if we train someone and then they leave for more money someplace else?" COO says, "What if we don't train them and they stay?" The logic here is so simple that it becomes funny when stated this way.

But it happens all the time. Rarely will you see a corporate-wide policy where advancement is predicated on achieving pre-defined training. And of course, a trained person needs to get paid more, even though the company paid for the training. That person is now more valuable!

This should be part of any corporate policy; train only those people you believe in, those who you feel will be much more productive if they are trained. And then only give out a raise if they do indeed achieve pre-set productivity goals. If they don't meet the goals, then let them leave and be someone else's problem.

Employee: *What? You mean left?*

A brand-new term is presented to the employee—he can only guess what the boss means by "Go starboard." The employee might know what starboard means, but this is the first time the term has been used in this situation. How is he to know whether the Boss knows what it means? The employee would love to follow orders, but he is genuinely confused and seeking clarification. The boss has some training of sorts when he talked to the consultant, and he should make sure that others get this training too.

Training should not be done in a silo; there should be an element of knowledge sharing involved. Companies that understand the value of training require that those who go to training, share some of their newfound knowledge—perhaps by giving a one-hour presentation or creating a document of helpful hints. This not only reinforces the training but will also demonstrate that the employee has learned something. Plus, others will gain knowledge too. Training should be more than taking a class; it should be an entire package, with clearly defined tasks, outcomes, and deliverables.

The employee should demonstrate eagerness and ability to do and learn more on his own. His role should have a pre-defined career path that enables him to progress up the success ladder without undue bureaucracy. Productivity and other measurements should already be in place. This way it will be easier to demonstrate that the employee is worth investing in and will highlight the improvement after the training. The knowledge transfers should be graded, by the attendees and the boss (yes, the boss should get some knowledge too).

It is no wonder so many companies don't like sending people to training. It's expensive, the employee may be gone for as much as a week, there is no measureable benefit, and the employee often quits within a year because he didn't get a raise (or, worse, he becomes disgruntled and he stays). This is why there need to be defined rules and processes around training, just as you would have for any new procedure.

Boss: *No. My left, your right. It's called "starboard."*
             Don't you know anything?

Even though the boss has just learned this stuff himself, he has probably convinced himself that anyone rowing a boat should know these nautical matters. This boss doesn't view himself as a mentor and presumably not as a teacher either. Too often, people get into a position of leadership without really understanding what takes place at that level, or at least not understanding what it takes to accomplish what is required to get the job done. This boss seems more like a project manager: he knows someone is supposed to do a task, has some idea of when it needs to get done, and then reacts when things get delayed. He doesn't show any real leadership qualities. Shouting out, "Don't you know anything?" is ineffective. The job of a leader is to mentor and instruct, not to berate.

Employee: *Okay, but the oar is on the wrong side. I'll have to stop and switch it.*

The employee has gone back to just stating the facts. (The "okay" here should include an exasperated sigh.) He only wants to "just do his job" and is getting frustrated by his boss's interventions.

Boss: *Okay, but hurry up; we are running out of time.*

Here's that exasperated-sigh-laden "okay" again. The boss too is getting frustrated. He keeps telling the employee what to do, but nothing is getting done.

Employee: *Okay, done.*

Just the facts. Nothing but the facts. Just doing what I'm told, just doing my job.

The process of "rowing to the islands" has totally disintegrated. Time has passed, efforts have been made, the employee is "working," a consultant has analyzed the situation, and yet there has been no forward progress. The problems started when changes were made, changes that were supposed to increase efficiency and productivity.

But why? Is the new oar defective? Is the employee resistant to change? No, it's not the oar nor the employee; in this case, the change did not come with any announcement, any training, or anything to prepare the employee. Changes are not only inevitable but are necessary in today's dynamic business world. However, preparation and planning are necessary. The old adage of "failing to plan is planning to fail" is never truer than when implementing change. People need a warning, an explanation, a reason, and (definitely) training.

When changes happen, human beings often need to "blame" something. Ever hear of the stages of grief? There seems to be a parallel psychodynamic response to changes, and one of those stages seems to equate to "blame" or a need for "a reason." In this case, it can be simply stated as the corporate need of competitiveness: "We must remain competitive. Therefore, we need better tools to do our jobs."

Until this need for a reason is fulfilled, it will be hard for employees to focus on their jobs. For changes to be as undisruptive as possible, people should be told the "reason" for the change, not just the change.

Boss: *But now you're going around in circles the other way! We need that consultant.*

Totally frustrated, the boss leans on the consultant some more. There is no discussion with the employee to figure this thing out, no opportunity for the employee to express any ideas. To have such a conversation, the boss would have to imply that he is doing something wrong. This boss doesn't want to discuss things that were going right or about past experiences in which he or his employee may have encountered similar situations. Simple questions like "What are we doing different today from days that things went well?" or "When did things start to go wrong?" can bring more insight toward finding solutions than most outside consultants can.

For this type of conversion to take place, the boss must first admit that he doesn't have all the answers. Then, he has to acknowledge that perhaps the employee knows more than he does. It is far more acceptable in today's world to just call in a consultant. That's one reason consulting is so lucrative.

Consultant: *What you need is a rudder and a helmsman at the stern (that's the back) to steer the boat in the right direction. I can sell you a rudder and get an experienced helmsman.*

After having some time to think about a solution, the consultant has figured out how to make some good money: Why just "consult" when you can also sell product and sell contract labor? Beware of the consultant who can solve your problem only by adding more costs. His consulting fees aside, he should be showing you how to be more productive or gain more quality with existing resources.

Adding people and tools is the simple solution. Everyone wishes they had more money and more things; however, to be profitable, you must be continually increasing productivity with the tools you already have.

Boss: *Wow! You really know your stuff. What else can we do? We are really behind our schedule.*

The boss is apparently more concerned with meeting deadlines than meeting project cost estimates, which he must not have. Where are the added costs for the helmsman and navigator coming from? Who approves these things? Apparently, nobody. Meeting the project deadline is its own reward.

Consultant: *Well, many nautical shops have a navigator at the bow with a compass, electronic sextant, GPS, and charts. It's industry best practice. I can get you those too.*

Certainly, it might be true that a large shipping company has these things as standard equipment, but does this company need these items? Just piling on more people and technology is usually not a solution. This boss can't even work out a problem with the number of oars, how is he going to deal with rudders, compasses, sextants, and such?

Lately, it seems that all one has to do is to declare something as "industry best practice" and everyone jumps on board. No one seems to ask questions like, "According to whom?" or "Where did you discover that this use of nautical equipment is industry best practice?" The main question that should be asked is "Yes, others might use these tools, but do we need them?"

"Yes, others might use these tools, but do we need them?"

Boss: *Do it. ASAP.*

The force driving the "meet the date" mentality is strong in this culture. There is no proof-of-concept, no return-on-investment analysis, no concern given to costs or budget. How can companies survive with such a culture? Where's the accountability?

Consultant: Cha-ching!

Throw enough money at anything and miracles can happen—and those miracles seem to benefit consultants the most.

"Throw enough money at anything and miracles can happen—and those miracles seem to benefit consultants the most."

Boss: *Get back to the dock. We have to start all over.*
We need a rudder installed. And make room
for a helmsman and a navigator and some
other equipment.

There are times when it is best to climb back down a mountain, reassess the best course of action, and start all over. But this isn't one of them. There must not be any real oversight to this effort, at least not by qualified people. If you're going to start over, the best thing to do at this point is change the boss and get out of the contract with the consultant for as cheaply as possible.

How much better would it be for this company if, at this point, the employee came back, picked up the two old oars, and continued on as normal?

How is this boss going to recognize what needs to take place in order to return to a more efficient process? He's the one who caused the time delays and budget overages. Don't expect a solution from those who caused the problem.

"Don't expect a solution from those who caused the problem."

Employee: *What? Why?*

Again, the boss has made changes without talking it over with the employee or communicating with the employee in any way. Imagine the employee rowing like crazy, thinking that with no input from the boss, he must be doing what the boss wants. However, in reality, the boss is in discussions with the consultant, making a plan that will undo everything that has gone before. How does this make the employee feel?

Boss: *Don't ask questions! Just do it. I have a consultant that knows what he's doing.*

The boss further insulted the employee not only by claiming that someone from the outside knows more than the employee but by implying that the employee doesn't know what he's doing.

Consultant: *Everything is installed and we are ready to go.*

Everything must be installed and ready to go. Consultants are never wrong.

Boss: *Okay! Everyone in the boat! Let's go!*

Not only is there no review or quality check, but the boss doesn't do any training or preparation. Not even a speech to kick off this new team. He is in a hurry, after all; besides, he's the boss. Everybody should just do as he says. He can't be wasting time explaining his decision to employees!

Employee: *There's not much room here—and the boat is pretty deep in the water. We are taking in water. It's hard to row.*

Still the employee just states the facts, offering no suggestions. Sounds totally like complaining. Notice that the added tools and added personnel goes unchecked, but there's also something else. Even though more people have been added to the project, nothing's been done to add more space. Now the risk of sinking is greater than ever before. Without proper planning and communications, things can actually get worse, not better, when you add people to a project team.

Boss: *Just go! We are way behind schedule! We need that consultant.*

After all these improvements, the boat still is not moving as it should. It must be the employee's fault. All he does is complain.

Consultant: *I can get a couple of guys from offshore. They have a master's degree in electronic engineering, but we trained them in rowing. They are really strong; one can row during the day, and the other can row at night. You'll need a second-shift helmsman and navigator too. Oh, I see water in the boat. You could use a bilge pump too.*

Recognizing that the boss is blaming the problem on the employee, the consultant follows the path handed to him and comes up with a plan to replace the employee and increase the number of consultants on the project.

Boss: ***Do it! We are behind schedule.***

Everything the boss has done was toward getting the project done ASAP, yet he is way past due and way over budget. You can't really say he is over budget; it doesn't seem as if there was one to begin with.

Consultant: Cha-ching!

The consultant continues to be successful; he has increased his monthly invoice!

Boss: *Okay! Everyone in the boat! Let's go! Toward that island! We need to get there yesterday!*

Again, just hop in the boat and go! That strategy of failing to announce a plan worked so well the last time, he thought he should repeat it. One difference this time: the boss states a goal that is totally unrealistic (get there yesterday) perhaps to get more effort out of the team.

Consultant: *Which island? We need a map. And some*
documentation on how you have been going to
islands in the past.

Those are all very good questions, which should have been asked before coming up with a solution. How can anyone come up with a solution without knowing where you are and where you want to go, and something that shows you the obstacles and available paths?

| **Boss:** | *I have an employee that doesn't understand this new technology. He can document what we used to do. Bring the employee back here to the dock. You manage the boat. We will stay here on the dock and document the process while you're rowing.* |

Did you notice when you first read this that the boss never did answer the questions, not even the important one of "which island?" The boss probably doesn't even realize that he gave the direction to reset the project and start all over again. Plus, without even meaning to, the boss just outsourced the entire rowing operation to the consultant (there should be another "cha-ching" in here).

Did you also notice that "where the business wants to go" (from the boss's very first line) is never defined? The project team grew from one rower on one shift to a team of helmsmen, rowers, and navigators on two shifts, yet the business objectives and return on investment (ROI) were never defined. Have you seen your department, or perhaps one that you work with, grow without justification? Perhaps there was justification, but you weren't told what that was. Keeping it a secret is the easy way to manage; you never have to expend the energy, and you can hide failures and claim them as successes!

Sometimes departments will buy "automation software" because it will make them more productive. Presumably, they will be able to "do more with less." However, in the end, they never seem to reduce their staff (and, in fact, they added people to manage the software), nor do they produce higher quality output. The goal of any change should be documented and well publicized.

Never is it mentioned what the deadline is or why there is a deadline. Most times, projects are started just because someone with political power demanded that it gets started, but they never state the reason (or never communicate the reason) to everyone involved. Again, this is easier; this way, no one can object or give their opinion on why this isn't a good idea or why there are plenty of other projects that are more important.

In the short run, it always seems easier, and it often is, simply to do as you are told and not rock the boat (pun intended). However, if you want to keep your company profitable, you must always be looking for that "overhead" that is stealing profits by costing money but not delivering value.

Employee: *Hey, what's this other rowboat with only one oar doing tied to the dock?*

Now that he is no longer mindlessly rowing a boat, the employee sees more new things that he never was told about. There are other tools available that might be useful, but he doesn't have a clue about what they are or why they are there.

Boss: *That's the DRB.*

More stuff that the boss knows that he didn't share with the employee.

Employee: *What?*

The employee does know what it is (it's another rowboat with only one oar); he just doesn't know why it's there.

Boss: *Disaster recovery boat.*

The boss just gives the definition, no other explanation.

Employee: *Can't I just use this oar and row the boat with two oars like we always did in the past?*

The employee recognizes that all this previous effort and money spent on consultants, contractors, and tools could have been avoided if he had simply been given this extra oar to begin with. He could give this information to the boss's superiors, but he has already been relegated to the dock to do documentation. Basically, he's been demoted—who's going to listen to him now? Besides, the boss's superiors are hardly going to admit that they let the boss go out and needlessly spend money. It's best for everyone to just keep going in this direction.

Boss:	*Don't you know anything? Are you still living in the past? We need to have a back-up in case the primary rowboat sinks. Besides, I have solved the problem: the consultants are succeeding where you failed. And now I have two rowers for that same price as one employee! Twice as far for the same price! I have improved productivity!*

More insults. The employee doesn't know anything and is thinking in the past, even though, in the past, boats were being rowed to islands by only one person instead of three. "Thinking in the past" is taboo, while holding on to ridiculous new ideas is acceptable. It's better to have backup equipment sitting idle than it is to use it. It's better to have three people in the boat than it was to have just one.

The boss is also proclaiming success. The consultant he hired is succeeding when no goal was ever stated. And the boss can point to one part of the system (the rower) and declare a success. There's nothing being measured that says the contract rowers are doing the same or better job.

Employee: *Hey look. I can stand in the front (or in nautical terms, the bow) and use this one oar to paddle the rowboat—umm, I mean DRB—on both sides like it was a canoe. And I can go pretty fast too.*

Without being constantly pushed to work harder, the employee is now free to experiment with the new equipment and discovers that he can indeed operate a boat with one oar.

This is the type of solution that the expert consultant should have come up with; this, or better, the fact that the row boat was built for two oars.

Boss: *Stop fooling around! Are you done with that documentation yet?*

That's all the boss sees—that the employee is fooling around. He does know he gave directions to do some documentation but hasn't been checking up on it. He has a boat full of contractors and an employee writing documentation nobody cares about. Do you think there may be an opportunity here to "do less, get more"?

Just imagine a restaurant kitchen with too many cooks. They are bunched up and bumping into each other, all working frantically to fill the order given to them; however, none of them is productive or meeting the expectations of the customer. Certainly, if you want more customers, you need more cooks, right? Or think of a restaurant manager who tries to solve the problem of constantly running out of clean dishes by hiring more employees to wash dishes. These are the same types of solutions many managers in today's businesses use to solve very common problems. It could be that the real problem of not having enough dishes is due to breakage or theft. The simple solution of buying more dishes will allow for the rush hours to have enough clean dishes, which can be cleaned during the slower times. Or perhaps the problem is antiquated cleaning equipment, or just an ineffective employee.

More cooks don't necessarily mean more customers can be served. Do you have enough tables, stoves, pots, pans? Dishes? It is a leader's job to identity what the real problem is and make the appropriate adjustments. How about raising the price? You will most likely get fewer customers, but you may get more revenue and thus higher profits ("Do less, get more"). When a manager is inexperienced (or, worse, has the wrong experience), he is likely to make the wrong changes. Ever see a successful restaurant expand its location or move to a bigger location just to go out of business a few years later? It happens all the time.

Employee salaries and benefits are often the costliest expense at any company. And they are the ones with the most flexibility, as the others are often fixed costs (such as debt or rent). Therefore, cutting employees indiscriminately is often the solution put forth by ineffective leadership.

Many companies are in the same position as our rowboat story. Three people in a tiny rowboat, all trying desperately to do their jobs, yet the boat is getting nowhere or is moving very slowly. Ineffective leaders start asking managers to "do more with less," and managers just tell everyone to work harder. This doesn't work, so more money is lost. Without ever considering that some managers may be very good at their jobs, poor leaders will issue the simple demand that every manager "must cut personnel by 20 percent." The problem is most likely that there are only a few managers who, like the one in our story, should be cutting 66 percent of their work force. But many of today's leaders were yesterday's inept managers; they have no successful experience doing the things they lead, so they can't make rational decisions on personnel and processes.

That doesn't mean they aren't capable of learning how to lead a competitive company. They just need to take a look at the people they lead—take a hard look. Going back to our story, what is the navigator doing? Is there a need to make continuous readings on current position measured against previous position and constantly preparing progress status reports? Think about your own department, are weekly status reports with precise cost-to-date and estimated costs to complete really necessary? Can your team be just as effective with brief weekly reports and a full review on a monthly basis? Take a look around. Are there any helmsmen on your team, and are they adding any real value? Can the rower look over his shoulder and see where he's at and just spend a little less effort on one side of the boat and get the correction required to stay on course? Do less, get more.

Look at the quality of your personnel. Does your company hire low-wage offshore contractors? Are you really saving money by paying low wages? Adopting a strict low-wage policy will probably result in your company being the training ground for your competitors. Your experienced contractors and employees (the really good ones) will seek better pay and move on to other opportunities. You will be left with new personnel and some experienced workers who don't have the self-confidence or ambition to seek a better wage (do you really want them working for you?). Plus, instead of focusing on the real goals of the company, they will spend their time training and fixing mistakes. If you had half as many employees who were motivated and experienced, could you get the job done? Perhaps.

Reward these good employees and pay them 50 percent more. You may need only half the employees and which results in a 75 percent reduction in payroll and probably get more done. Do less, get more. The point here is that you have to ask these questions, solicit solutions, and try new things. If you have a large enough staff, particularly across many locations, you may be able to have a small test group and find out if you can do less and get more, one team at a time.

What if you're wrong? Is your corporate culture one that allows experimentation and understands that it's okay to make mistakes? If not, are you going to be like the employee in the rowboat or the employee fooling around on the dock to become the employee sailing off to a new job?

Originally there was only one boat, two oars (until the manager replaced them with one new oar), one rower, and one manager. This grew to two teams, each with a helmsman, navigator, and rower, plus a rudder and navigation equipment.

Certainly, the single rower version was an example of "Do less, get more." And if they had used two *new* oars, they would have been much more productive. Look around and talk to your team members. Ask them about how things used to be. What worked? What didn't? You have a wealth of knowledge on your team. They know their jobs and they know how to apply previous work experience to their current duties.

They may remember the days when they had two oars, or when they paddled a canoe, meaning they know how stand at the bow and paddle with one oar.

Another lesson from our story is that the rower isn't facing where the boat is going. He sees where he's been and uses that view to understand whether he is on course. He's pretty much heads down and working. He may need to look over his shoulder to check on progress, but if he does, he will slow down or move a little off course, so he needs to keep fixed on a landmark or something notable from his past.

While it is true that you should look to the future and not dwell on the past, if you don't learn from the past, you are likely to continue to make mistakes. Choose your landmarks wisely. Make sure they are clear and large enough to see from a far distance and not something that is moving or changing.

Employee: *Hey, look. I can tie my shirt to this oar to create a sail and let the wind blow the rowboat. And I'm going really fast!*

Again, the employee must say, "Look at me." It seems he has become invisible. He could probably just lay low and play with all the tools that are lying around. After all, who reads documents anyway? Even though the employee has basically "checked out," he does want to show the boss that he has learned something new and wonderful, things the expensive consultant never came up with.

Think how much better this company would be financially, while delivering superior value, if only this one boss had used both of the new oars and kept the old oars as backup in case of an emergency. The employee would be rowing the boat three times faster with half the effort (assuming this is even true about the new oars). The extra value being provided would be faster delivery time, and the employee would be freed up to learn new things (like sailing instead of rowing). Prices could be lowered, which would then lead to more customers. Instead, costs go through the roof, and there is no improvement in delivery times.

It won't take long before some start-up comes along and starts stealing business. "Well, they have lower overhead" will be the excuse. Rarely do you ever hear, "Well, maybe we have too much overhead." If you want to help your company be more profitable, then you should always be searching for that new process, procedure, or methodology that helps you and your team to do less and get more.

Boss: *I told you to quit fooling around; you haven't completed the documentation yet. You're fired!*

The boss, true to his ineptitude, has concluded that this employee is useless. He has everything he needs to prove to HR that the employee must be fired. Never mind that the employee demonstrated methods of improved productivity or that the boss has quadrupled expenses and has been continuously late on delivery. It's the employee that is the problem. The boss will probably get kudos for not having to pay severance and for lowering costs when he did not replace the employee.

It has become far too commonplace in today's corporate world to "reorganize" a company. Wall Street may look favorable upon an announcement that the company cut 10 percent of its workforce or has reduced expenses by moving a portion of its labor to another country. But do the Wall Street analysts ever check to see if any of that actually worked? Do they ever ask, "How did you get in this mess in the first place?" or "Why should we trust you now?" Well, to be fair, there are times when stock prices go up slightly after an announcement of major changes, but the price usually returns to its previous level because no real benefit was created.

Terminating an employee has a devastating effect, not just on the employee and his family but to the employees who are left to continue the work. It may also affect the relationships that the terminated employee has with customers, and of course the company must replace a knowledgeable employee with someone new or, worse, with no one.

Leaders often dismiss the value that long-time employees bring by using terms like "tribal knowledge" or dismissing the loss with statements like "Well, they kept all their knowledge to themselves. We're better off without them." Terminating an employee will cost a company far more than just the severance package and retraining of replacements.

Nobody ever measures the costs of the mistakes made when the company lacks an experienced person to do the work. They also fail to assess how much business is lost because of broken relationships (both in sales and in operations).

Employee: *Too late, I quit. I got a job with a sailing company.*

This is an example of a win/win/win situation: The consultant made lots of money and has an indefinite engagement as the resident expert in all things nautical. The Boss got a promotion for solving nautical problems. And the Employee found a new career sailing instead of rowing.

The lessons here are simple. It is very important that every company understand the motivators that are driving their personnel, whether they are contractors, employees, or management. Certainly, each one of them is looking to make a living, and most are looking to better themselves both financially and personally. But are they really looking out for what is best for the company? What does your company have in place to ensure that their work, their decisions, results in better profits? How is that measured? What does "success" look like?

As mentioned in the introduction, if any of the behaviors highlighted in this story are happening at your company, you are one step closer to improving your company's profits. The next step is much more difficult: initiating that change. The change in processes may result in the difficult decision of letting people go. However, if your company isn't constantly evaluating all roles and all personnel, the company may soon no longer exist at all.

FINAL THOUGHTS

This whole situation with the rowboat plays out time and time again at corporations everywhere. It seems that the company that doesn't operate this way would have an extreme advantage over its competitors. Yet, it continues to take place.

When the company that made Blackberry cell phones announced it was laying off thousands of people in 2013, it was hard to imagine what those people did for a living. Sure, they worked hard and believed they were doing the right thing, but the Blackberry device itself was built overseas. What were the people at the headquarters doing? What were these people working on? Were they all "helmsmen and navigators"? And the people doing actual work, were they just outsourced rowers doing what they were told?

Think of the companies that replaced the Blackberry. Are they rowing with both oars? Or perhaps have they matured past oars and are now sailing? Do you get the feeling that they too have been hiring helmsmen and navigators lately? What's the next big thing? When was the last big innovation? Why aren't the prices of mobile devices going down?

Understand that in the story, poor management is the cause of high overhead and excessive costs, but there could be good reasons why people and processes were originally added, and these reasons may no longer be valid. Whether your company is highly successful or has seen better days, it always makes sense to evaluate your processes. All too often, the manager who makes changes that reverse his early decisions is viewed not as an "continuous improvement" leader but as a failure that has to constantly reinvent his team. Don't let that happen! Let your peers and your leaders (and their peers) know your intention is not to reverse your bad decisions. On the contrary, make sure they understand that you are building on your past successes and are always in a state of "continuous improvement."

Another piece of advice is not to go overboard (pun intended). Don't overdo a good thing. The legendary golf instructor Harvey Penick said it best in his *Little Red Book:* "When I tell you to take an aspirin, please don't take the whole bottle." What he's saying is, just because one little change had a successful outcome, this doesn't mean that this is the right change for everything and everybody. Harvey goes on to explain, "In the golf swing a tiny change can make a huge difference. The natural inclination is to begin to overdo the tiny change that has brought success. So you exaggerate in an effort to improve even more, and soon you are lost and confused again."

This is true with business processes. We've all seen large companies report significant improvements in their bottom line simply by moving a call center to an offshore facility.

However, moving all call center personnel to the cheapest country will start working against the company's goals of customer satisfaction, greater revenue, and increasing profits. An executive level VP once presented how much money the company was saving by comparing US call center rates with foreign rates and multiplying that by the number of call center personnel. Great savings in costs were highlighted. The presentation concluded with, "And that's it. We can't reduce costs any further."

Really? This is a high-level leader? All they did was move all the call centers to the cheapest possible outsourcer. Metrics such as the number of call center personnel before the move compared to after, or the percentage of personnel compared to revenue, were not part of the presentation. Nor was there any mention of what the company was doing to reduce the number of calls in the first place, or what the main drivers of the calls were. And never was there any mention of the quality of those calls. Was the customer satisfied with the experience? Were they likely to continue to be customers? There was so much more room for improvement that it was difficult to hear, "We can't reduce cost further."

Successful companies don't just focus on direct costs. They focus on profitability, which includes customer satisfaction and reducing the number of steps or touch points required to deliver a good or service.

Do less, get more. That's what this story is all about, yes it displays a boss that is doing more and getting less, but the intention is to show the opposite. It can't be over stressed: do less, get more. This is very important toward delivering greater value while remaining competitive.

"Do less, get more."

Here's another analogy to strengthen the "do less, get more" philosophy. Let's imagine a profitable home builder. This builder has a large fifty-acre development of two hundred homes. As you watch the process, you will see that a specialized team comes in and digs the hole and builds the foundation, then moves on to the next lot.

Next, a framing team comes in and builds the wooden structure, before moving on to the next lot. Specialized teams come in to install electricity, plumbing, roofing, insulation, windows, and many other phases that require specific skills.

It may take up to six months from digging a hole to moving in, but the builder is able deliver fifteen to eighteen houses per year. While it certainly is possible to build a house "from hole to move-in" within a month—if you put all your laborers from each phase of the project all at once, fifty people putting in the foundation, then wood framing, and roofing, siding, and all the other phases all at once—everyone will be working on top of each other, bumping into one another and losing efficiencies, not to mention that safety will be compromised.

There are builders that will do this as a "rush job" to satisfy a demanding customer. However, with this process, the builder might only build twelve houses a year. And just how much quality is in each house when you have foundation people helping with electricity? Plus, what is the cost? Fifty people working for a year building twelve houses costs a lot more per house than fifty people building eighteen houses in a year.

The successful builder is the one who has found that "magic" number: the right number of foundation workers compared to framers compared to roofers and so on. It doesn't help to have four people build a foundation in three days when it takes six days to frame a house. It's better to have two people build a foundation in six days so that the foundation is ready when the framers are ready to start. The whole process is much more complex than what is described here, but hopefully you get the point.

Doing less—in this case, using two people to build a foundation in six days—produces more (more profits) than four people building a foundation in three days. Every process, every company, has a "magic number." It is the job of managers and leaders to work with their employees to find their magic number to remain competitive.

REFERENCES

Penick, Harvey, with Bud Shrake. *Harvey Penick's Little Red Book: Lessons and Teachings from a Lifetime in Golf.* New York: NY Simon & Schuster, 1992.

Hindle, Tim. "The Hawthorne Effect," *The Economist.* November 3 2008. http://www.economist.com/node/12510632.

"BlackBerry Job Cuts: Smartphone Maker to Lay Off 4,500," *The Huffington Post Canada.* Updated 09/20/2013. http://www.huffingtonpost.ca.